"And England h Ashes"

The untold, behind the scenes story of England's victory in the 2005 Ashes Series – the greatest Series ever!

David Clarke

Dedications

To my wonderful wife whose patience, support and most of all unconditional love makes everything possible

My Dad, no longer with us - when he was he could never quite come to terms with the fact that his "lad" shared the odd glass of red with Beefy (his hero)

My Mum who still thinks I am 10 years old and need to be looked after by her – love you Mum!

Contents

Preparing the Ground

Back in 2005 I was the Event Manager for the England and Wales Cricket Board (ECB). I was responsible for working very closely with each of the major international cricket stadiums and various other organisations to ensure that the Board's showcase events were delivered to the highest standard possible.

I had to oversee the delivery of the cricket itself. This included working very closely with the ICC Match Officials and the management teams for both England and the team which was touring. Keeping our broadcasters happy (never an easy task) was also a priority, as was working with the stadiums to improve spectator facilities and the safety and security measures which are an essential part of any major sporting event. Making sure that our spectators had the best entertainment we could offer was a further aspect of my job.

I had previously been part of the communication team at ECB but stepped up into the event role (no one within ECB ever officially appointed me but they were very happy to let me get on with it) after personally witnessing possibly the worst ever day for English Cricket at Edgbaston on 7th June 2001. On that evening England played Pakistan in a One Day International – I was there watching with a colleague. The match will be remembered not for any amazing feats by players from either side but for the mindless violence and vandalism wreaked by a section of Pakistan fans who invaded the pitch threatening the safety of players, officials and sending shambolic images of cricket in England around the world.

Although we were not at the ground in any official capacity John (the colleague who was with me) and I very quickly got caught up in helping the club deal with the chaos. It was very apparent that the people running the club were completely unprepared for what had happened and totally overwhelmed by the media frenzy that followed.

It was following the events of that night that I decided I needed to do whatever it took to make sure there was never any repeat of those scenes at an English cricket ground. Sadly there was not enough time to bring about changes before two more matches; one at Headingley the other at Trent Bridge; were subject to similar disgraceful scenes. At Headingley a steward suffered serious injury as he attempted to protect the stumps. I will never know how we escaped without worse injury at Trent Bridge as elderly stewards were lined up in front of Stanley knife wielding youths in a bid to keep them off the pitch!

Something had to be done and done quickly.

In the next couple of months with Home Office representatives, senior police officers and people from several other agencies, I drove a major review of crowd management at cricket stadiums. The results provided us with some shocking revelations. With one or two notable exceptions there was a completely "laissez faire" approach from grounds – the view frequently expressed was "this is cricket; we do not have a problem".

Well we did have a problem and we set about putting it right.

Three years later – back to Edgbaston and the 2004 ICC Champions Trophy. I was the Tournament Director. Possibly the biggest game in world cricket; India v Pakistan, was one of the games we had to stage. Lots of people told me that I was crazy for recommending that the game be played at Edgbaston given what had happened there a few short months previously. I was confident that we had changed things around and, working with the team at Warwickshire County Cricket Club (the ground owner), we could hold the game successfully.

Result – a party! The game was held against the backdrop of a capacity crowd with both sets of fans having a great time with no trouble whatsoever.

The measures we had put in place clearly worked and to this day there has not been any repeat of those ugly scenes of 2001.

I remained the Board's main contact with the police and Government on safety and security matters. The drastic measures we had put in place after 2001 once again became a focus of attention and came to play a critical role later in that summer of 2005 having a key impact on the outcome of the Ashes Series.

In the previous five years I had the privilege of spending a significant period of each winter overseas touring with the England team in a media management role. I became a part of the "England Bubble" which Duncan Fletcher so meticulously engineered and maintained to give his players the right environment in which to perform at their best. I had seen at first-hand how Fletcher, firstly with Nasser Hussain as Captain, turned England from a "rabbit" for the majority of nations into a team that was extremely hard to beat every time it took to the field. Then with Michael Vaughan taking over from Nasser, a team of genuine, bona fide competitors at every level of the game. This gave me a huge advantage over many of my colleagues (including, in my opinion, many in the Senior Management of ECB) in that I got to know the England Coach, Captain and many of the players on a personal level and understand what support they needed from the off-field team.

At this stage I must hold up my hands and confess to being a huge fan of Duncan Fletcher and his coaching style. As a coach in a different sport I am acutely aware of how difficult it is to get players from varied backgrounds and levels of experience to come together and form a single minded unit focussed on the needs of the team rather than those of the individual. As far as I am concerned creating the environment for those players to thrive and perform at their very best was Fletcher's strength.

To put it very simply, I was at the heart of everything associated with any international cricket played in England both when it came to every aspect of the staging of the matches and in terms of the atmosphere in the dressing room.

So far as the 2005 Ashes were concerned, I firmly believe that this gave me a unique insight into the events which unfolded during the course of that astonishing summer.

It is this insight which I would like to share in the following pages.

Oh that little Urn……

Florence Morphy, formerly of Melbourne Australia, has an awful lot to answer for in the world of international cricket, if we are to believe the official history of the origins of The Ashes Urn.

The one time music teacher from Melbourne was one of a group of ladies who presented the then England Cricket Captain, Ivo Bligh, with a small wooden urn containing (or so the legend goes) the ashes of one of the bails from the England v Australia Test Match which had just finished – a match England won to win back the Ashes. This was during the England tour to Australia of 1882/83 when Bligh had vowed to bring back "the Ashes"; this he duly did, much to the dismay of Australian cricket fans – at the same time the Ashes legend began!

Miss Morphy clearly made a big impact on the England captain who, incidentally, also happened to be the son of the sixth Earl of Darnley. Very shortly after they met Miss Morphy became Mrs Bligh and later the Duchess of Darnley following her husband's inheritance of the title.

The Earl died in 1927 and following his death his widow presented a terracotta urn to his former club, the Marylebone Cricket Club (The MCC). The urn is purported to contain the original Ashes which were presented to Mr Bligh by Miss Morphy and her friends in Melbourne in 1883 - the fate of the original wooden urn is not clear!

Thus began the saga of the small terracotta container which began life as a personal gift to a successful England Captain but then became one of the most intensely sought after symbols in world sport and a generic term for any sporting competitions involving England and Australia.

What the Duchess could not have seen nor predicted when she presented the urn to the MCC was how it would become the symbol of so much national fervour, sporting endeavour and, indeed, political intrigue in the sporting world.

What began as a generous gift to a loved one's private club has become the central focus of a struggle for power between the Club and the recognised, properly constituted, broad-based governing bodies which currently run cricket across the world.

Never was this intrigue and tension more fundamentally revealed than in the days leading to the final day of the final test at The Oval in September 2005.

A quick history lesson – up to the early 1960's the MCC was the dominant controlling body of cricket in England and across the world. It was responsible for choosing the England Team, arranging tours both in England and overseas. The Club's power was absolute throughout the game – even the very Laws under which the game was (and continues to be) played were controlled by the MCC. This was clearly a situation which could not last and when the Labour Government of Harold Wilson was elected to power in the UK in the late 1960's the writing was on the wall.

It was Wilson's Government which introduced public funding for sports bodies. Under no circumstances was any funding going to be put in the hands of the MCC as it was a private club and as such it could not receive public funds.

As a consequence the Test and County Cricket Board (TCCB) was created to administer the professional game and the MCC Cricket Association became the National Cricket Association (NCA) to look after the recreational game and receive cricket's government support.

As a result, cricket started to receive financial help from the Government and the power of the MCC began to decline.

11

To this day the MCC remains the most famous cricket club in the world and owns the iconic Lord's Cricket Ground, for many "The Home of Cricket".

The recent history of cricket however is littered with incidents which suggest that various elements within the Club have still not moved on from those days.

Even the most cynical and sceptical non-cricket lover had to accept that the 2005 Ashes Series had captured the Nation's, indeed the cricketing world's, imagination in a way in which no other series had ever done. Such was the passion of the crowds and the feedback from the television and radio audiences that it was very clear to me that one image and one image only would be a fitting climax to such a wonderful series.

That image would be Michael Vaughan the England captain holding aloft the Ashes Urn at the end of the Oval Test Match.

The challenge, one which probably turned out to be the biggest challenge of my professional career, was to persuade the hierarchy of the MCC that the Ashes Urn could be a part of the final series presentation which we were planning as the climax of The Oval Test Match.

After the astonishing events at Trent Bridge during the fourth Test Match it was very evident that an England series victory would be the likely outcome – this added to the impetus and urgency to get our MCC colleagues on side.

As I expected at the time our original request was met with a very clear and uncompromising "NO" from the MCC. The justification being that when the Darnley family had given the Urn into the MCC's care it was as a personal memento and family heirloom not as a sporting trophy. It was also added that at no stage had the Urn been the official trophy of any series between England and Australia. A few years earlier the MCC had in fact commissioned a beautiful Waterford Crystal Bowl which was presented to the winning captain. Whilst the Bowl was an excellent addition it did not come close to the real prize – the Ashes Urn.

On the face of it these were legitimate reasons, however, in my view, it is difficult to divorce these reasons from the fact that it would be someone from ECB who would be handing over the Urn as part of the presentation party. Under no circumstances would the ECB hierarchy tolerate someone from the MCC sharing the same platform.

And thus you have it: England's cricket success and the Nation's desire to celebrate that success would be marred by a deep chasm in the game which had existed since the 1960s – a sorry comment on the game's hierarchy indeed.

As you can probably deduce from the TV pictures of the time and photographs which were splashed all over the press, I did not accept this initial position and continue to pursue the matter. Several, somewhat intense conversations took place at various levels within both organisations in an attempt to reach a compromise situation.

At one stage it was suggested to me in a private moment by a senior MCC official that, as I would be on the stage at the end of the match, they could give me the Urn to keep in my pocket to quietly "slip it to Michael" so that he could celebrate with the rest of his team and hold it aloft for the photographs.

Frankly I really couldn't believe what I was hearing. That such an icon of the sporting world could be the root cause of such division and that certain individuals were prepared to treat it with complete disrespect to achieve, what I perceived as, their own political goals was astonishing.

Following that conversation I realised just how deep the impasse we were at was. I went away and produced a compromise solution which I thought would satisfy both parties.

On the one hand ECB and its broadcast partners, photographers and everyone else who was desperate to see the England captain lift the Ashes Urn at the end of a successful series. On the other hand was the MCC, determined that the Urn was not to be physically presented so as to protect the status of the Ashes Urn as a "non-sporting trophy" and respect the wishes of the Darnley family.

As with many solutions to complex apparently insolvable problems the solution was simple and elegant (even if I do say so).

I suggested that we created a plinth to be placed on the centre of the post-match presentation stage with the Urn placed on that plinth prior to the final ceremony. Then at the given time the England captain (it could have actually been Ricky Ponting as at that stage the outcome could still have been drawn series) would step forward and raise the Urn - so simple but so effective.

A simple solution which, thankfully, no-one was able to resist - we had our solution.

Sports fans would never believe how complicated and sensitive these things can be. All I ever wanted to do was to get the Urn in the Captain's hands and get the party started; competing against this was the needs of sponsors, broadcasters, photographers and by no means least egos of a range of important people who very much have their own agendas on such occasions.

Some years prior to 2005 and only after numerous "cock-ups" when the wrong things were given to the wrong people, I decided I needed to be on the presentation stage so that I could hand the right trophy to the right person to make sure it got into the right hands. This was never a problem until Mr Collier arrived on the scene. He made it very clear that he "did not think it appropriate that an employee (i.e. me) should be on stage at such a prestigious event". Despite my protestations that I was only there to make sure things were done right he was not to be moved. I will leave it to you dear reader to work out who took over that responsibility!

However, as it happened at The Oval the sheer number of trophies and other paraphernalia to be presented was such that there was no room on the stage. So we set up a table slightly off stage so that I could hand the appropriate trophies to the Chief Executive and he could ensure that the right presenter gave them to the right person. Guess what? Thing still got messed up as the newly created Compton Miller Man of the Series Award was handed to the wrong person to present to Freddie.

Such is the nature of professional sport!

The Build-up

Imagine this if you will. In 2005 I had been working at the heart of English cricket for approximately 15 years. During that time I had never witnessed a home victory in an Ashes Series! I cannot begin to tell you just how demoralising that could be at times.

In fact it was 20 years since England had last won a home series and 18 years since England had held the Ashes (Mike Gatting's side was the last to win in Australia in 1986/87). In the intervening period we had watched as England teams led by England greats including David Gower, Graham Gooch, Michael Atherton, and Nasser Hussain were put to the sword by the dominant Australian sides.

On more than one occasion the England challenge had capitulated embarrassingly and frankly the England team, not unreasonably, became the butt of many a comedian's jokes. All too often it was a very painful experience admitting that I worked in English Cricket.

In the years leading up to 2005 I had also come to realise how thoroughly professional the Australian tourists were every time they arrived on these shores. Without exception, the Australian psychological onslaught against England was underway even before the players arrived, whether it be a trip to Gallipoli or to the Somme to pay their respects to Australian war dead or the PR war waged by Steve Waugh when England were struggling to find a captain. The Aussies were always on the front foot and playing attacking shots before a single ball was bowled.

England on the other hand would typically be very British about the whole thing and not indulge in such tactics.

In the latter part of 2004 I felt very much that it was time for the off-the-field team at ECB to play a much more supportive role and help give the England team an edge if at all possible. I had an advantage over the majority of my colleagues as I lived through and could remember that famous England success; the fabled series of 1981 otherwise known as "Botham's Ashes" and the impact that series had on the nation.

If I needed any reinforcement for that view it came in South Africa in December/January 2004/05 when England played magnificently and achieved a series win against that formidable South African team. The final Test Match of that series was one of the most dramatic that I was ever involved in as England took on South Africa in Johannesburg. The England support from the "Barmy Army" was fantastic and probably instrumental in lifting the players to win the match and the series.

More than ever before Johannesburg emphasised to me the impact that great support can have in helping a team cross that fine line between winning and losing.

I had a very strong belief that 2005 was the year for the Ashes to come home for the first time in my career and for the first time in the memory of many supporters.

I knew that we needed the 2005 Ashes Series to stop the nation as had the 1981 campaign.

To this end I pulled together a group of colleagues from the ECB commercial and media team's in October 2004. Most of those colleagues were too young to have a detailed memory of Botham's' series but they all bought into the proposition that we should aim for the 2005 Ashes series to "stop the country".

So it was from that moment that we began to look at ways in which we could put together a great series of Test Matches whilst at the same time supporting the team and hopefully giving it an edge.

In the months before the Australian team arrived plans were put in place aimed at providing as much opportunity for fans to see live broadcast of the games through dedicated "fan parks". We also set about making sure that the welcome our visitors got every time they walked on the field was as patriotic from an England perspective as possible.

Then there was the "Guard of Honour"! On the face of it an innocent piece of ceremonial where children from the area local to each ground were invited to line up either side of the players gate with flags to welcome the teams. This appeared to irritate the visitors several of whom took to avoiding walking through the flags in what the English cricket media quickly began to see as very churlish behaviour. This farcical behaviour reached a climax at Edgbaston where it was impossible to avoid the walk and media reports suggested that

Mathew Hayden was heard to swear at one of the children as he brushed aside the flags. This was very much to the amusement and delight of the England party who realised that things were beginning to get under the skin of one or two of their opponents.

As has been said before many times the margins between success and failure at that the very highest levels of sport are incredibly small – any advantage could only be positive.

The Australians arrive

When asked to list my top five sportsmen of all time it would look something like this:

1. Mohammed Ali – (can anyone doubt this?)
2. Michael Jordan – (basketball was my first love)
3. Steve Waugh (yes an Australian)
4. Bjorn Borg (so dominant at such a young age)
5. Billy Bremner (what would you expect from someone whose life growing up was watching the "Mighty Leeds").

Steve Waugh's place in this group is as much down to his mastery of the psychological aspect of international sport as it is to his undoubted ability and tremendous captaincy skills.

It was Waugh who introduced the practice of taking the Australian team to historical sites to commemorate Australian heroes of World War I when he took his group to Gallipoli.

Ricky Ponting and Coach John Buchanan adopted similar team bonding tactics in 2005. The squad arrived at Heathrow one day, only to climb aboard the Eurostar for a trip to the Somme the very next, for a visit to a part of the Somme region in France where the local community has sworn they will 'Never Forget Australia'.

The town of Villers-Bretonneux owes its existence to the formidable courage and resilience of the Anzac forces that liberated it. Freedom came at a terrible cost, however, with more than 1,200 Australians killed at this beautiful place.

Whilst Australia were bonding as a formidable group through shared patriotic experiences the England team were being fired up in a London hotel by ex-Royal Marine and adventurer Alan Chamber MBE FRGS. The same guy who had motivated the England Rugby team to victory in the Rugby world Cup a few years before; unfortunately I wasn't privy to his chat but whatever he said it certainly worked.

Jerusalem

Let's face it, you either hate it or you love it!

I love it and so did the team and the Coach – the music, the voice of Sean Ruane and the fantastic videos produced by Sky Sports to the music that became an essential ingredient of Ashes Cricket that summer.

Was this a happy accident or careful planning? In truth it was a mixture of both.

The concept of playing a piece of inspirational music with a video at the start of each day of Test Match cricket had its origins in a conversation between me and my colleague Joe Bruce in early 2003. Joe was under pressure from the sponsorship manager of Npower, the company sponsoring Test Cricket, to persuade ECB to introduce the National Anthem at the start of each Test Match.

Right here I need to make one thing very clear for the avoidance of any doubt. I am as proud of being

English as anyone could be however, I really could not see and still cannot see any place for our National Anthem at the start of Test Matches. I can hear the roar of protest and accusations of being unpatriotic but my stance was based on two very pragmatic and, self-evident facts.

In the first instance it was historically very rare for there to be a substantial crowd in a venue prior to the start of play; having both sides lining up on the outfield whilst the national anthems were played to an almost empty stadium did not seem appropriate to me and in many ways it felt more disrespectful than not playing the anthem at all.

The second and probably most important point was something I had realised whilst working with the team.

Anyone who has the opportunity to witness the intense preparation that goes on both in the dressing room and on field ahead of a Test Match particularly for the opening batsmen cannot help but understand the pressure to be prepared and focussed for those first few balls that are going to head their way at the start of a game. Maintaining the focus and concentration in preparation of facing 90 miles an hour plus deliveries would be severely tested by having to stand through national anthems.

We did, however, need to find a solution which would satisfy our sponsor!

I very quickly saw an opportunity to solve two problems at the same time whilst also providing another means of support for the team.

One of Duncan Fletcher's pet hates was the scenario where England players would be preparing on the outfield for a Test Match or One Day International whilst at the same time in the background our broadcast partner would be showing highlight packages from previous matches (or the previous day's play). Invariably the highlights would show England wickets falling and the opposition's batting successes. To illustrate I can clearly recall watching Marcus Trescothick preparing to open the batting at a Test Match at Old Trafford as a video montage was on the big screen just behind him showing him getting out. The players never complained directly but it really was a gift from the ECB to any opposition given the difference between success and failure at the highest level of sport.

Fletch was very strongly of the view that the English game was effectively shooting itself in the foot by undermining its player's preparation by showing these negative images.

So we had a sponsor requesting some type of "pomp and ceremony" ahead of the first days play coupled together with a very unhappy Head Coach.

My solution to Npower's request was that:

"That we introduce a patriotic, motivational piece of music accompanied by a video of positive affirmative images of England in the field to be played at the start of each day".

Joe was able to persuade Npower that this was a good option whilst I was able to work with Sky Sports producer Barney Francis who agreed to put together the video.

This little package made its debut on the first day of the England v South Africa Npower Test Match at Edgbaston in 2003. To say the reviews were mixed is probably an understatement. Several members of the cricket press were very critical whilst a senior board official actually asked me "David, please tell me why we are playing a working class anthem at Test Match cricket?"

What really mattered though was that Fletcher, Vaughan and the rest of the squad loved it, as did our sponsor, so Jerusalem was here to stay. That is in every stadium other than Lord's – the MCC were true to form from the outset and refused to allow Jerusalem and the accompanying video to be played.

We did have quite a battle on our hands in the early days holding back our sponsor. In their desperation to put their mark on everything associated with Test Match cricket Npower wanted to print song sheets to hand out to the crowd and to encourage the crowd to "singalong" to Jerusalem. I resisted this as I was keen to see whether or not the project would develop its own energy (no pun intended) over time without us trying to bludgeon spectators into participating.

The press coverage at the time would also have you believe that Npower were behind the introduction of Jerusalem as the anthem for Test Cricket and believe me a couple of the company's main people were very busy taking credit. This is one of the "joys" of working with such aggressive commercial partners sadly.

Going into the 2005 series, plans to play Jerusalem were the same as for previous series; we would have a new video for each match which would focus on England successes from the previous match and we would continue to play it at the start of every day as the England team took to the field.

The MCC refused to come on board with the concept using the "we are not allowed to play amplified music" excuse, which was frankly wearing more than a little thin at the time. Consequently there was no Jerusalem to inspire England for the first Test Match; we had to wait until Edgbaston for the second match in the series to play Jerusalem for the first time.

The third match in the series was due to be played at Old Trafford. A few days before the game I received a call from Jim Cumbes the Chief

Executive of Lancashire County Cricket Club. The conversation went something like this:

"Clarkie, Jim here, - let's get to the point! As you know I hate Jerusalem! I really don't like it being played in the way that it is; but I have a good mate who is a music agent - he has asked me if we would allow a young tenor he has on his books to come along and sing Jerusalem on the first morning"

And so it was that I first met Sean Ruane the young tenor in question. As arranged he turned up on the first morning of the Old Trafford Test Match prepared to sing Jerusalem.

We had in the past utilised singers to perform as interval entertainment during international fixtures and to be quite honest it had been something of a disaster. Consequently I was a little dubious about how we were going to make the most of Sean on this occasion. Cricket stadiums are such big stages that it is very easy for an individual or small group to get lost and have no impact whatsoever, also we frequently had problems with the technology.

Given this previous experience I suggested to Sean that he go and position himself in front of one of the main spectator stands with a microphone and sing there. He did and the response was terrific! Very quickly we had the majority of the stand singing along to Jerusalem as the video played and the team took to the field.

I managed to catch up with Duncan later in the day, he was delighted. As a consequence we booked Sean for the rest of the Test Match and he continued to get the same response.

Time for a cliché!

How many times have we heard the cricket coach, football manager or other such sportsperson utter those magical words "Win the winnable's"? Well, we had a winner and I could see very definitely that it was one that we should continue to use. Very quickly I was able to secure the budget and get in touch with Sean's agent to book him in for as many days for the rest of the series as we could.

At this stage it would be easy to say the rest is history; Sean continued to sing, the crowd continued to join him and, what's more, driven by the Barmy Army, Jerusalem became the anthem for the Team and the Series.

As each day went on, every England success was heralded with a chorus of William Blake's famous hymn.

The England squad loved every minute of it. Ahead of that fantastic finale at The Oval Michael Vaughan asked the nation to support the team:

"The backing of the country is like having a 12th player on the field," Vaughan said.

"And the thought of having the whole country singing a song as emotive as Jerusalem is

something that will get the boys stirred up just as we come on to the field."

Such was the extent of the passion generated around series we arrived at a unique situation which only a few people ever knew about. We found out some months later that the Australian squad was well and truly shaken by the atmosphere at the Oval. On those crazy tension filled days at The Oval the Australian team was so traumatised by the patriotic fervour filling the ground they could not leave the dressing room until Sean had finished singing.

Strangely Sean did appear to take longer to finish as the days went by!

I guess you could say that the off-field team had achieved their ambition of helping the on-field team to a famous victory!

In truth, we will never really know but what a great thought – the tough, no nonsense Aussies traumatised by a hymn!

Later in these pages I will talk about the events surrounding the Trafalgar Square party and the role that Sean and Jerusalem played in that.

For now, however, I want to tell you about one of my most treasured possessions. Hanging on my office wall as I write this is a framed photograph of the team in Trafalgar Square signed by the England Captain with the words of Jerusalem on one side and the results of the Ashes series 2005 on the other.

Just in case I ever need reminding of those heady days!

The 2005 Australia tour of England was probably one of the most congested of any tour which had ever arrived.

In all there were three separate series during the summer in addition to the various county warm-up matches that the tourist played.

First up there was the NatWest Series which involved England, Australia and Bangladesh. Immediately after this was the NatWest Series which featured England and Australia. Finally, there was the main event; the five match Npower Ashes Series.

In the opening match of the Series Bangladesh rewrote the history books by beating Australia in the first match at Cardiff.

That result was not repeated in the Series and by the time the teams had played each other twice it was England and Australia who arrived at Lord's to contest the final which (very unusually) ended in a tie.

And so it was onto The NatWest Challenge, a three-game series between the two old rivals the first game of which was at Headingley on 7th July 2005. A date indelibly etched into the memories of most of us as a result of the horrific incidents on the London transport system that day.

Being a son of the broad acres (Yorkshire that is and yes I know another cliché!) Headingley was always a little like going home for me and that day was no different. The day started much the same as any other One-Day-International at Headingley with a large very vociferous crowd, many of them wearing some of the most outrageous fancy dress you can imagine. Quite what the processes is where a normally rational human being wakes up one morning and decides to get dressed up as a bunny girl (in most cases at a minimum weight of 16 stone (224lbs) and travel to a cricket venue on public transport to watch a match whilst getting totally legless just escapes me, but I guess it is all great fun at the end of it.

And so it was at the start of the day. But by the end the atmosphere in the stadium was very different.

Shortly after 11 am I got a call asking me to go to the Stadium Control Room as the police match commander wanted to see me. As I arrived he began to explain to me that there was an a major police incident happening close to the stadium (it was in fact an armed bank raid) with lots of roads closed off and various other measures put in place. He was very keen that we prepare a plan to hold spectators in the stadium during the interval between innings to keep them away from the incident.

In itself this was a unique situation and would have presented us with a considerable challenge. It was very much a custom at Headingley for spectators to go to one of the several pubs in and around the stadium during the interval break so keeping a couple of thousand fans in the ground would have been difficult. In the end though the problem did not materialise as the incident was over before the interval in the match so the local pubs enjoyed the patronage of a number of England fans.

However, throughout my conversation with the match commander I was having great problems concentrating on what he was saying. This was nothing to do with my lack of attention or his delivery!

Immediately over his shoulder was a television, on this TV pictures were showing thick black smoke coming out of a tube station in London and images of a seriously damaged bus. There was no sound to the pictures but it was not necessary – it was clear that something very serious was in process in our capital.

Over the next couple of hours the cricket at Headingley became academic as news of the magnitude of the incidents in London spread through the crowd and into the dressing rooms. In many ways the match became inconsequential as the events in London unfolded.

It was hardly surprising that the Australian party were extremely concerned about these events. Many of them had their families with them and they had stayed behind in the team hotel in central London. To compound matters the remaining two matches in the series were due to take place at Lord's three days later and at The Oval two days after that.

I spent much of the remainder of that match contacting ground authorities at Lord's and The Oval, the Met police and senior ECB management. On the ground both the Australian team management and the ICC Match Referee were becoming increasingly concerned and needed reassurance.

Naturally, under those evolving circumstances it was not possible to give them any cast-iron guarantees that everything would be okay, but we were able to persuade them that the series should continue and the team should not return to Australia as several of the party were saying they wanted to.

It was clearly a very difficult time for the Australian squad and its management. A number of the players were so concerned they made public comment about wanting to return home.

Very quickly that day I arranged top-level meeting at ECB offices at Lord's the following day involving senior police figures, government representatives, MCC staff, the Match Referee and Australian team management. The meeting was very much about providing reassurance to the teams and officials that the two grounds were well prepared and everyone would be safe and secure.

In reality we had been living with the threat of terrorism for a number of years, especially following the events in New York in 2001. Since the Twin Towers tragic attacks every aspect of security around major gatherings of people was the focus of huge attention from police and other security officials – cricket stadiums were no exception. Over the previous two to three years we had put lots of training in place, held exercises to test how well we were prepared and generally raised the ability of every stadium to run matches safely. Lord's and The Oval were two of the best at that stage. Deep down I knew that we were as well prepared as it was humanly possible to be and that the matches must go on – otherwise we would have lost the whole summer of cricket and a small group of fanatics would have won the day.

The safety teams at Lord's and The Oval working alonside the Metropolitan Police and a very professional stewarding company both had excellent track records when it came to managing their stadiums in a safe and secure way. Thanks to that, coupled with the recent experiences and the police support available, we were able to satisfy everyone that the remaining matches could go on and that the families would be safe in London.

Decisions such as these are always extremely difficult, particularly when large numbers of people are involved. The moral debate is always difficult – should a sports event go ahead when so many people had been killed or seriously injured? On the other hand, should the event go ahead at any cost to show that the terrorists could not win? For many involved the natural instinct was to withdraw and cancel anything which may become a target.

In truth the remaining matches had to go on otherwise terrorism would have won out in the City of London and all of its residents would have been victims yet again. Defiance in the face of threat was the overriding requirement.

Reference to Wisden, Cricinfo or any of the other keepers of cricket's archives will show that both games were played in front of capacity crowds and that Australia recovered from losing the first match to win the remaining two thus clinching the Series.

No amount of words or pictures will ever go close to portraying the incredible effort which went into ensuring that for the spectators and players it was "business as usual".

And so to the action

First Test - Lord's, July 21-24

Whilst the Safety and Operational Teams at Lord's were always excellent, matches at the home of cricket were always a challenge from an ECB perspective.

Uniquely amongst cricket grounds the MCC is adamant that matches held there are their matches and they will run them accordingly. The home of cricket in NW8 is a wonderful place and without doubt one of the best places in the world to play and watch cricket, but it was always very much a case of managing things in a very diplomatic way to ensure that ECB requirements were met without creating tension with the MCC.

The atmosphere on that first morning was electric! The place was full and ready to go from the outset. Steve Harmison was unplayable, hitting several players hard before drawing blood with a delivery which hit Ricky Ponting on the helmet. This incident was very significant as not a single England player moved to check if the Australian Captain was ok – the rules of engagement were very clearly stated at that moment!

England bowled Australia out for 190 before tea.

The anticipation amongst the England fans was tangible to say the least, but then along came Glenn McGrath – by the end of his post tea stint England had been reduced to 48 for 5, they were in real trouble.

Reality check delivered you could say!

The rest of the match went the tourist's way as they won by 239 runs with McGrath proving unplayable.

The England bubble was well and truly "pricked" along with it mine too – I was now looking again at yet another Aussie celebration sometime later that summer.

Second Test - Edgbaston, August 4-7

For many reasons Edgbaston has always had a special feeling for me! The next five days did nothing whatsoever to change that situation.

What an amazing match and what an incredible start. An errant cricket ball, possible the world leading pace bowler not paying attention and boom – Australia went into the match without their spearhead! McGrath stood on a ball during the pre-match warm up, had to be carried off on a stretcher and was out of the match with a twisted ankle!

What happened over the next five days will never be forgotten, especially by those who were fortunate enough to be there and watch events unfold first hand. Without doubt Edgbaston hosted one of the all-time great Test Matches over those five August days in 2005.

The action for real started at the toss – Ponting won the toss and decided to field. If you get chance watch the video and look at Michael Vaughan's face – he is definitely struggling to contain his delight that England will get first use of the pitch and, more importantly bowl last!

The fans who turned up at Edgbaston over the next five days were treated to an amazing feast of the best that Test Cricket can deliver. England rattled up 400 on that first day, including a stand of 103 in 17 overs between Andrew Flintoff and Kevin Pietersen.

On the second day Australia progressed to 88 for 1 before Ricky Ponting attempted a big sweep against Ashley Giles only to miscue and be caught out. Before the end of the day Australia were all out for 308. Almost the final act of the second day was one of those amazing dismissals which had become Shane Warne's stock in trade - Andrew Strauss bowled padding up to a leg-break that turned two and a half feet. Shades of Mike Gatting at Old Trafford!

England were up against it on day three being reduced to 72 for 5, cue Freddie! Flintoff proceeded to mount a brilliant counter-attacking innings, ending up last man out for 73 in a total of 183.

In that score he hit two superb straight sixes, the second of which had I been a little braver I might have caught as it landed on the roof of the Pavilion close to where I was standing. It just so happened that I was standing exactly in the same spot as I had been a year previously as I watched the India v Pakistan match in the ICC Champions Trophy end with both teams shaking hands and walking off in safety – a target I had set everyone after the 2001 scenes at the same venue.

Great memories indeed!

Despite Freddie's heroics the lead was only 281 and the game was only at its half way stage - Australia had two and a half days to get the 282 runs they need to win. Cue Freddie yet again (sometimes I do think that the 2005 Series should have been christened the Flintoff Ashes – just as '81 is often referred to as Botham's Ashes). In one famous over Freddie bowled Justin Langer and then had Ponting caught behind. Then at the end of the day Steve Harmison served up what for him was a very rare offering; a superbly executed slower ball which had Michael Clark completed fooled. It was Australia that had the problems at the end of the fourth day.

The final unforgettable morning arrived with Australia starting the day at 107 for 8 needing a further 107 to win – England needed the little matter of two wickets.

Never before or since have I been in a stadium where such an incredible tension built throughout a session of play. A packed house crammed into Edgbaston and I challenge any one of them to say there were not expecting a short morning, Freddie knocking over the two wickets required and home for Sunday lunch! I know I was!

How wrong we all were and how quickly and dramatically the mood changed.

First of all Warne and Lee edged the Aussies towards their target until, with 62 still needed, Warne was out in that most bizarre and unfortunate way, "stepped on wicket". Brett Lee was joined by Michael Kasprowicz and the two continued to edge Australia closer until almost without anyone noticing Australia were one hit away – 3 needed.

The controversy over what happened next continues to rattle around today - Harmison to

Kasprowicz – short ball, Kasprowicz attempted to get out of the way only for the ball to glance off his glove and be caught behind the wicket by Geraint Jones.

Game over. England win by two runs, the Series is level, absolute pandemonium everywhere – in the stands, the commentary boxes and on the field.

Subsequently slow motion replays suggested that the batsmen's hand was off the bat handle in which case he should not have been given out. However, umpires in 2005 did not have the benefit of the Decision Review System and everything happened at a speed which made it almost impossible for the umpire (Billy Bowden) to see.

For my part, I had watched that whole morning unfold from right behind the bowler's arm in the Players' Dining Room in the old pavilion at Edgbaston. Sadly, in some ways, the building no longer exists; otherwise I could have shown you the threadbare carpet where I paced back and forth willing someone to get those last two wickets!

Maintaining a professional detachment (usually a perquisite of the job) was never tougher as the tension built and built. As much as I wanted the team to win I also knew that an Australia win would effectively seal the Series and kill the public's interest in the remaining three matches.

The stakes were huge, and I really did not want to watch another Aussie celebration party in an English Test ground.

By the time the teams lined up for the third match of the Series at Old Trafford, four days later, the DVD of The Greatest Test was already on the shelves and selling well.

Third Test - Old Trafford, August 11-15

By the incredibly high standards set at Edgbaston the third Test at Old Trafford was almost a mundane run of the mill affair.

McGrath was back but clearly not 100% fit – probably needed at least another Test to fully recover!

The England Captain scored an excellent 166 (this after being bowled by his nemesis Glenn McGrath when on 41 only for "No Ball" to be given).

The England bowlers, led by Simon Jones on this occasion, used the conditions to bowl with radar-like reverse swing. They were so effective that it took a tremendous effort from Shane Warne to get Australia past the follow-on score. Without the batting efforts of the world's best leg spin bowler Australia would have been asked to "follow on" for the first time in around twenty years – so dominant was the England attack.

By the end of the fourth day England had an insurmountable lead and Australia a full day to bat out the draw.

Traditionally very few, if any tickets are sold in advance for the fifth day of Test Cricket because matches often finish in four days or there is very little cricket left to play on the final day.

On the rare special occasions a game is poised at such a remarkable stage that the public's imagination is captured and thousands decide to turn up "on-spec" to see if they can get a ticket.

This was one such occasion! Literally thousands turned up only for many to be disappointed as the ground was full and the gates shut by 8:30am. The unlucky thousands who were turned away had to make do with sitting at home and watching the day unfold on TV. The visitors managed to salvage a draw at Old Trafford but it was very clear that

England had the real momentum as the teams headed to Trent Bridge.

I have to confess that I was not at the ground for that last day or indeed for the entirety of the Trent Bridge Test Match. I had long since promised my wife and three young daughters that we would have a family holiday each year irrespective of who England were playing and what was happening. Today it is usual to refer to this sort of thing as getting ones "work life balance" in order; to me it was a simple and very easy choice!

Much as I loved my job it was just that family came first – no competition! What's more in ECB's Sally Brooks there was the perfect person to take over so I could leave safe in the knowledge that all would be ok!

As it happened, I may have been away in France for a couple of weeks but I became the focus of attention for just about every Englishman there –

the interest in The Ashes was at fever pitch even on the South West coast of France.

Holiday over and back home I watched the final acts of the Trent Bridge match on TV. It would have been easy for me to go to the ground and be a part of it all first-hand but frankly I preferred to stay away. Trent Bridge and I never really got along even though most people think of it as being a wonderful venue. The place had been one problem after another for me particularly with the management regime that had been in place there until very shortly before that summer.

However, the old ground in Nottingham was the backdrop to a wonderful second win for England – the post-match scenes so diametrically opposed to the cavorting Shane Warne performing on the players' balcony as on previous occasions. I was very happy that we would not be subjected to that display again.

England leading an Ashes Series 2 – 1 with a very real potential to clinch a Series win – surreal for me to say the least and things were very quickly to get even more surreal if that was possible!

The Mayor Wants a Party

When I got back to ECB towers on the Tuesday following the amazing events at Nottingham the ECB's Head of Communications, Colin Gibson, asked to see me as soon as I arrived.

I was aware that Colin had been heading up a small "task force" entitled "Project Victory" throughout the course of the Ashes Series, however I did not know the details as I was not involved and frankly the Ashes was all-consuming for me. Colin told me that the ECB Chairman had had a call from the office of the London Mayor Ken Livingstone the essence of which was that "Ken wanted a party to show that London was open for business" this was of course a direct response to 7 July bombings.

The Mayor was offering Trafalgar Square for a celebration should England win the Ashes; he was offering a day after the final day of the final Ashes Test or a date some two weeks later. In very simple terms Colin asked me if I could do this.

I recall asking what the alternative was with his project victory. This involved a victory parade in Birmingham with an open top bus running from central Birmingham to Edgbaston Stadium where there then would be a concert and various other activities to celebrate. All this was scheduled to take place in two weeks after The Oval.

It was as they say a no-brainer: one of the nation's premier iconic places the day after what we hoped and expected would be a triumphant outcome for the England team versus an event some two weeks later in the Nation's second city.

The only answer was of course let's go with Trafalgar Square. From that point on my life did not belong to me for the next 16 days.

One of the first things I had to do was to meet the Mayor's staff and various other people to discuss how we were going to stage this event. I went along expecting a group of maybe half-a-dozen people, only to be met by a room full of around 40 people representing an incredibly wide range of interests from the river police to the department in charge of rubbish bins to the City of London Police.

Right from the outset it was made very clear by the Mayor's representatives that whilst Ken wanted a celebration he was also adamant that the City of London must not be disrupted from its normal working day.

The Mayor's people were very clear that the discussions regarding the celebration should be confidential and that on no account was there to be any prior publicity – in the minds of all concerned England's victory parade was to be a purely spontaneous affair.

Having met with the various London authorities the ball was now well and truly rolling. Amongst the myriad of component parts in place was a huge question regarding which companies should broadcast the event. At the time ECB's contract with Channel 4 was due to come to an end with the last ball of the Oval Test Match. Various people within the organisation who had been responsible for looking after the Channel 4 relationship assumed that we should invite the channel to cover the celebration. I had a very different view of this as I was aware that BBC was very interested in becoming a broadcast partner and that Sky were very keen to partner with BBC.

As far as I was concerned there was no discussion to be had. On the one hand there was Channel 4 with very little in the way of available outside broadcast resources and, indeed, who cricket had chosen to end its relationship with. On the other there was BBC with its vast experience and resources when it came to outside broadcast along with ECB's very innovative partner Sky Sports.

After a short but fairly intense discussion common sense prevailed and BBC with Sky were invited to broadcast the proceedings. Once this decision had been made there was the little matter of putting together the logistics of a full outside broadcast – to this day I remain convinced that without the expertise of the BBC this would have been impossible.

Whilst these things always appear to be pretty simple and straightforward to the TV viewer, to anyone who was actually there at the time something like this is actually very complex. Fortunately we were able to draw on some excellent experience of various organisations which had staged events in Trafalgar Square before. I had a first class team working with me on presenting the Test Matches; a team which I was determined would assist me in delivering the celebration.

Shortly after the decision to go with BBC/Sky the story began to leak that a major celebration was being planned should England retain the Ashes. The Mayor's team were far from happy that the story was out there but there was little that could be done at that stage.

It was pretty clear that the story was being "leaked" by several individuals connected with the Channel 4 broadcast team and could probably be summed up as being an act of sour grapes.

Many of those involved with Channel 4 were naturally very unhappy that the Channel's cricket coverage was about to end – in truth, however, the Channel had demonstrated for some time that cricket was not a priority. It is not widely known that the reason ECB moved the start of Test Matches from 11am to 10:30am was to ensure that a day's play would be completed by 6pm to facilitate Channel 4's newly acquired broadcast of "The Simpson's". In addition even during some of the most tension packed days of that Ashes Series the Channel had left its cricket coverage to cover horse racing.

The relationship with Channel 4 had certainly waned since those fantastic, innovative early days.

Whatever the source of the leaks, the outcome was inevitable as interest in the Final Test and what came afterwards continued to mount hour by hour.

That crazy last Test!

Fifth and Final Test - The Oval, September 8-12

Let's just say that the build-up to the Oval Test Match was a crazy time. Meeting after meeting at various bars, offices and restaurants in and around Trafalgar Square had to be attended. At the same time we had to deal with an incredible demand from public and media for access to The Oval; broadcasters from across the world were clamouring to be at the match.

Such was the demand to be at the match that for the first time ever in English cricket we had to introduce new measures to ensure that only the people who were actually working on The Oval, be they broadcast, press or other suppliers could gain access otherwise the ground would be overcrowded. A special accreditation put in place without which entry to the stadium was impossible.

One adventurous Met Police officer discovered how well this process worked when he attempted to get in by showing his warrant card – he was suspended for attempting to abuse his position.

And of course there was that presentation to be organised!

Thursday, 8 September 2005 duly arrived and with it began six of the craziest and most dramatic days England cricket had ever known, either before or since.

After four days of the best entertainment live sport can deliver it all came down to the last afternoon of the last day of the last Test. England needed to bat out the final day and the Ashes would be their's. Australia had to take ten wickets by late afternoon leaving themselves enough time to score however many runs were required to win the match and draw the Series. It was that simple.

As on each of the previous four days I spent much of the last day hastily travelling to and from Trafalgar Square, as we tried to finalise the last minute details with the Mayor's Office and a multitude of other people who had a role to play. All this against a backdrop of "will it happen or not". Would England win the match or at the very least secure the draw they needed to bring the Ashes home?

The final day dawned with England 34 for 1, a lead of 40 runs – simple calculation: Australia needed to get 9 more wickets as cheaply and quickly as possible – England needed to bat as long as possible and score enough runs to make an Australia win out of the question.

During that morning session England lost two wickets to Glenn McGrath, leaving them at 68 for 3 then calamity struck for the Australians. Shane Warne, one of the safest pair of hands in world cricket dropped a catch from Kevin Pietersen. It has been said that Warnie "dropped the Ashes" when that ball hit the ground – I guess we will never know, but it certainly inflicted a major dent in the Aussies efforts that Monday morning.

I was oblivious to the detail as I was locked away in a meeting in a restaurant just off Trafalgar Square – we were planning how the media would be handled the next day, even though we really did not know how many or who would turn up and of course whether any of us would be needed at all.

I left that meeting just after lunch with things far from settled – the game could still have gone either way.

By tea "KP" had scored his first ever Test Match century and went on to score 158, effectively batting Australia out of any chance at winning the game.

When England were all out during the evening sessions the Australians were left with the impossible task of scoring 338 from only 17.2 overs (that 104 balls to score 338 or 3.25 runs per ball!

It was never going to happen and everybody knew it, but....

Cricket being cricket it has a set of rules to play by and on this occasion the rules required Australia to take to the field and begin their innings.

Four balls in and the light was not great – the Umpires invited the Australian batsmen to leave the field as per the rules when visibility is poor! Not surprisingly Langer and Hayden (Australia's opening batsmen) did just that.

The atmosphere in the ground was charged to say the least – everyone, to a man, woman and child (including the Australian team and supporters) knew that The Ashes were coming home, but any celebrations were on hold as the game still was not over.

At this stage the Umpires, Billy Bowden and Rudi Koertzen were still out in the middle of The Oval monitoring the light situation – yes if the light had improved the rules would have meant that Australia would have to come out and bat again no matter how futile that would have been.

As you may suspect, I was acutely aware of the situation – a stadium full of fans, a worldwide audience of billions and an England team willing the match to be finished. Some might think it a privilege, others a bit of an overwhelming responsibility, but it fell to me to go and talk to the umpires in an attempt to find out just exactly what was going through their minds at that stage plus when and how was the game going to end!

A peculiar thing happened to me on the way to the middle of the pitch as I went to talk to the umpires my phone was in my jacket pocket and it began to buzz signalling an incoming call – as I went to answer the "unrecognised number" the buzzing stopped immediately. I never gave that little incident much thought until several years later when I bumped into an old friend and former colleague who told me a fascinating story which underlined just how massive and worldwide the focus on that last day of the series was. Warren was the Event Manager for the International Cricket Council (ICC) based in Dubai; along with the majority of his colleagues and a bar full of other "ex-pats" he was in one of those fabulous hotels that Dubai is renowned for watching the proceedings on a big screen.

The level of frustration amongst everyone watching was such that Warren (according to his version) announced that he was going to find out what was happening at which point he dialled my number. As he hit send he looked up at the screen to see me walking out to talk to the umpires and reaching into my pocket to take his call – he very hastily cancelled the call when he saw that I was "busy". An amusing story but more than anything it underlines the astonishing level of attention focussed on events on that September Monday afternoon in Kennington.

Back to the Umpires – they were adamant that it would be some time until they could consider a premature end to proceedings, as they had to stick to the ICC Regulations. At this juncture, with no immediate prospect of an improvement in the light situation, the Umpires left the field for the sanctuary of the Umpires' room in the Pavilion at The Oval – I followed them!

As you might appreciate, I was very keen to get to a situation where the match could be concluded and the celebrations could begin in earnest – and we could give release to the tension which had been building in the Stadium all day. But Rudi and Billy were bound by the Regulations and were not for shifting from their stance – that was until the ICC Match Referee Ranjan Madugalle appeared.

Ranjan immediately told me that he fully understood my position and told Rudi and Billy that we were going to go and see the Captains (with both Captains agreement the match could be brought to an end). Hidden from the sight of broadcasters, spectators and just about anyone else who was interested in the outcome, the small delegation of ICC Match Officials and myself arrived in the players' dining room. The dining room is behind the dressing rooms at The Oval, Ranjan asked both Michael Vaughan and Ricky Ponting to come and meet us (Ranjan insisted that it was these two only as it is the Captains' decision).

It is worth adding that I was being pursued by the floor managers from both Channel 4 and Sky together with a representative of BBC Test Match Special at this stage for news of what was about to happen – I asked each one of them to wait outside the players' area until we had something definitive to share with them.

Not unnaturally, Michael Vaughan was very quick to agree with Ranjan's suggestions that the Captains "shake hands" and agree that the match was over, Ponting on the other hand was (equally unsurprising) reluctant to agree and asked for time to return to the Australia dressing room and consult with his team and management.

As Ricky left the room Shane Warne came in the other direction looking for something to eat – he immediately went to shake hands with the England Captain and congratulate him on a Series win. So as far as "Warnie" was concerned the match was over, the best side had won the Series and brought the Ashes home – he was more than a little incredulous that his Captain had gone to consult – it was over!

I was very clear about how I needed things to end and it was not in the time honoured way where the Officials let the team know then the rest of the world finds out via the Public Address System or TV or Radio! A Series that had exceeded all others in the cricket world eyes demanded a fitting finale.

I spoke with Michael Vaughan and asked him to make sure that any celebrations by the team be kept in the dressing room and away from public view (assuming of course that the Australians agreed to the match ending) until a formal end was announced.

Then I persuaded the two Umpires (being "entertainers themselves to a degree this was quite easy) to walk out onto the field and "ceremoniously" remove the bails and uproot the stumps to show the world that the game was over, the result was a draw and England's long wait was over – the Ashes were coming home. Once I had their agreement I spoke to Channel 4 and asked them to focus their cameras on the Umpires as they came out and then briefed Johnny Dennis to make the announcement over the PA.

And so we achieved those iconic pictures of Koertzen and Bowden marching out to the middle and removing the bails as JD announced "and ladies and gentlemen, England have won the Ashes".

What a perfect conclusion to an amazing series full of incredible sporting action, tension and drama. Removing those little pieces of wood heralded mayhem! Celebration in the stands, the dressing room and in homes, bars and clubs across the Country – The Ashes were coming home!

Very quickly, the customary post-match formalities were put together and the Trophies delivered, interviews took place and finally Michael stepped forward and lifted the Urn from the plinth under a downpour of confetti and choruses of Jerusalem!

The pictures I had visualised and fought so hard to achieve spread across the world as cricket fans everywhere (except perhaps Australia, for obvious reasons) celebrated the best series ever. It was very apparent that everybody's second favourite team appeared to be whoever was playing Australia judging by the outpouring of congratulations for the team.

Incidentally, every Ashes Series since 2005 has ended with the Urn being lifted in the same way. A battle truly worth fighting I think!

After a riotous lap of honour the team made it back to the sanctuary of the dressing room to begin the real business of celebrating their achievement.

For me and my ECB colleagues there was time for a short celebration before clearing up the mess from the presentation and then on to Trafalgar Square. A few last-minute details to attend to, minimal sleep, and off to the Square for 5:30 the following morning to make sure we were ready.

Trafalgar Square and Freddie's Party.

Ken wanted a party – he most definitely got one!

I had finally managed to get the ECB Chief Executive to sign a contract for the hire of Trafalgar Square at around 5:30pm on that last day. Only then was I able to give a range of contractors the go ahead to begin building a stage, installing seats, sound systems, screens and a whole range of other paraphernalia we needed to run things in the Square.

To this day, I must confess to being stunned at what followed on that Tuesday in Central London. I got to the Square at around 5:30am to find lots of England fans already there in their England shirts with banners and music - most of them had very clearly been partying all night and decided to come to the Square for the best kept secret in London.

Time for a small confession, on my way to Trafalgar Square I will never forget picking up a text message from my colleague, Andrew Walpole who was the team's Media Manager, the text read something along the following lines:

"The Sun has a special wrap-around this morning carrying the words of Jerusalem – you should be very proud".

Believe me I was!

My team were in place and ready to go! One of my fondest memories of the day is meeting with Steve Agyei, Corrado Cecere and Kevin Bannerman and of course Jonny Dennis – the voice of cricket - to go through the plans for the day. This was the core of the team that I had worked with for several years as we went about transforming the presentation of cricket to the English spectator. It was a privilege to work with such a competent, highly committed group who each shared my passion for both the game and what we were doing. To this day, I remain extremely proud of the enormous achievements we made during the period we worked together.

Steve and Corrado were responsible for providing equipment and putting together the logistics whilst Kevin was responsible for our sound systems and running the show (he is Australian by the way, but that never got in the way of his professionalism). Any of you who attended an England cricket match during that period have been familiar with Johnny's voice on the PA but he was rarely seen.

Johnny asked me what I wanted him to do and how I wanted him to run the day, I responded by effectively telling him that he was a professional and to run it as he and Kevin felt appropriate. At that stage none of us knew what to expect over the rest of the day so it was pointless trying to be too prescriptive about things.

The transformation in the Square from the day before was amazing, by early morning we were all set up and ready to go and the crowd was building by the minute. In fact it just kept on building and building.

Estimates for the crowd that turned out in London that day have varied massively – all I can say is that there was not a space to be had in The Square or the surrounding streets.

The team were scheduled to leave the hotel at around 10 AM, my colleagues from the ECB Commercial Team had arranged for two double-decker open top buses to be prepared with the sponsor branding to carry the players and the rest of the party. This included players from the men's and women's England teams, family, backroom staff, broadcast crews and of course the inevitable hangers on who managed to gate-crash proceedings.

I do remember calling Andrew (Walpole) at about 10 - 10:30 AM to check how things were going! His response was the first real indication of what we had on our hands.

Andrew told me that the roads around the hotel where the team was staying were jammed with people. We soon began to get reports that the entire route from the hotel to The Mansion House, which was the first call, and then onto Trafalgar Square was packed with people all waiting to share the celebration.

The feedback from BBC and Sky was that the streets of London were in fact going to be closed as a result of the Ashes party – Ken Livingstone would get his celebration and show that London was in fact open for business but his desire to keep the City running as if it was a normal day had long been consigned to the bin. No matter!

There were so many things to remember and celebrate that day, doing justice to them is a real challenge. There are, however, some that I really must share with you.

As the buses with teams on moved towards Trafalgar Square we were able to keep an eye on the progress thanks to television monitors. We entertained the crowd in Trafalgar Square using big screens that we had installed.

Once we got the message that the buses were about to turn into Duncannon Street on its approach to the Square it was time for Sean to open up with Jerusalem. The response was incredible the entire crowd filling the square burst into song as the buses, surrounded by police motorcycle outriders, crossed into the Square and moved to park behind the stage.

The emotion in that charged atmosphere was tangible. I was told afterwards by a long-standing member of the BBC crew that in all her years of outside broadcast which included royal weddings, and the Olympic celebration she had never ever experienced such an emotional atmosphere. One that had brought her to tears!

So we had the buses with the players, we had the crowd and we had Freddie!

I will not go into Mr Flintoff's legendary condition as many better writers than me have written tomes on the subject. Let's just say that I was waiting at the doors to the bus as the players disembarked – as Freddie was getting off I recall saying "Freddie please give me that child before you drop her" he was very happy to hand me his little girl. So there I was! Standing in the middle of the England party and everything else going on holding young Holly Flintoff while her dad went off to complete THAT INTERVIEW. Fortunately Freddie's wife quickly came to the rescue so we could get on with the rest of the proceedings.

Shortly after the teams arrived I got a call over the radio from the person in charge of the security team. The conversation went something like this:

Question: "Do you know someone called Brian Lara?"

Answer: "Yes I do. Why?"

Answer: "Because there is someone here who says he is Brian Lara and he would just like to come and congratulate the players. What would you like me to do?"

At this point I went to investigate. Sure enough there was Brian Lara standing behind a barrier in the middle of a large crowd of cricket fans. It appeared that he had been on his way home to the Caribbean when he realised that the celebration was going on and decided on the spur of the moment that he really would like to pass on his congratulations to the team.

Of course we brought Brian into the backstage area where he met with a number of the players. I have to say that it was a real privilege to see the camaraderie and affinity between top-class international sportsmen, albeit from competing nations. The warmth and sincerity of the greetings from both Brian and a number of the England players was an honour to witness.

We did have a plan for the Trafalgar Square proceedings and a fairly tight time frame. Needless to say, these were now out of the window. When the team eventually left for their appointment with the Prime Minister at Number 10 Downing Street they were more than a little behind schedule.

Finally we managed to get on the buses ready to leave and again Sean took to the stage and got the crowd to join in with Jerusalem as the players went on their way.

After we had got rid of the team and most of the crowd it was time to head back to Lord's – we were all invited to a reception in the Long Room as part of the celebrations. To be perfectly honest, I was too tired and drained to get excited at that prospect but went along anyway.

The highlight of that little soiree for me probably sums up much of what had gone before – though I do need to edit the dialogue a little:

Freddie: "Eyup" Clarkie you alright mate?

Me: Yes Freddie

Freddie: What am I doing now Clarkie?

Me: No idea Freddie

Freddie: (Expletive) .me Clarkie if you don't know how am I supposed to?

At that point I put him in a taxi back to the team hotel though I have every suspicion that England's premier all-rounder of the day has no recollection whatsoever of that conversation but it rounded my day of nicely.

And so ended the most incredible six days that anybody associated with England cricket (no matter how remote the connection) has ever or indeed will ever experience. For my part, it was far and away the highest point of my career and will probably remain so as it is hard to believe that such events will ever be matched.

In many ways those involved in running cricket currently have my sympathy as I seriously doubt they will ever have the opportunity to enjoy such wonderful experiences again.

To this day, I will never understand why it was that over 100,000 people took to the streets of London to celebrate an England cricket team winning a series against Australia. Maybe it was the "18 years of hurt" which had gone before, perhaps it was a result of all the hard work in PR world and live broadcast that had enabled the Nation to witness every twist and turn of the series, or perhaps it was a reaction to the tragic events of 7/7! Whatever the reasons, our Nation and our Capital City showed very clearly that it was in fact "business as usual" and that we had a half decent cricket team to celebrate for the first time in many years.

That whole 2005 Ashes summer was amazing from beginning to end.

As with all tremendous high points low points inevitably followed, particularly when I came to learn that the ECB Chief Executive who had condoned everything that we had done and had taken a very active part in the celebrations decided that we had probably overdone things. His was not a widely held view but it was, nonetheless, a quite important one. I have to say that the whole thing had its own momentum and I will never really understand that change of heart. I suspect strongly that it was a politically driven decision aimed at preserving relationships with Cricket Australia.

The Final ECB Days

If 2005 was the highest point of my relationship with cricket, what came along in the years that followed was anything but!

Petty jealousies and a desperate thirst for power from a few individuals resulted in Duncan Fletcher's position being totally undermined and the team performance plummeting to a level that a resulted in a 5 – 0 whitewash in Australia in 2006/07. There are those who put this down to Fletcher failing and a number of key players having peaked in 2005 – personally I strongly believe that had Fletcher been allowed to continue managing the team in the way he had done in the build up to 2005 things would have been different. In that period the team had been free from political interference – the regime that had taken over in early 2005 was, frankly, incapable of allowing that to continue.

On a personal level my professional life hit a downward spiral as it became very clear that I, along with other long standing members of ECB, was on the new CEO's "hit list!"

He and I had not seen eye-to-eye on a number of occasions during his time as Chief Executive at Trent Bridge and I will always be convinced that he was envious of my relationship and role with the team. In reality I was powerless to fight the games being played by the CEO and his newly recruited ambitious hatchet man who proved very quickly that he was also ruthless in delivering the bosses and his own agenda!

It all ended for me in 2008 – three dismal years culminated in an errant email on Friday 13th June 2008 - followed by a Legal Agreement between myself and ECB, the contents of which I am not supposed to disclose...

Maybe, just maybe, that is another book. Who knows!

In the meantime, however, things turned around for me after a couple of years.

I now have the privilege of plying my trade with a great team of highly committed and passionate people at the fantastic Edgbaston Stadium during the English summer and travelling to India to help run stadiums in the Indian Premier League during the off season.

I appreciate that the IPL may be controversial in many ways to many people, but for me it has been nothing but an amazing experience. I have met and had the pleasure of working with many highly committed and thoroughly professional people both young and not so young.

Not a bad life after all!

The ECB "Off- Field" Squad

As with the success on the field the "off-the-field" success was only possible because of the single-minded teamwork of a small group of committed people. It is highly appropriate that I acknowledge and congratulate all concerned for a job so very well done in those few crazy weeks in 2005.

I am sure that there will be someone who I have forgotten – put it down to the march of time! If that is you my sincere apologies:

Colin Gibson	Head of Communications
Sally Brooks	Event Team
Andrew Walpole	Team Media Manager
Clare Fathers	Media Management
Joe Bruce	Commercial Manager
Mark Pearce	Commercial Team
Kiki Thompson	Commercial Team

Printed in Great Britain
by Amazon